GRATITUDE

Oren Safdie

BROADWAY PLAY PUBLISHING INC
New York
www.broadwayplaypublishing.com
info@broadwayplaypublishing.com

GRATITUDE

Cover art by Sylvia Haber

First edition: November 2020
I S B N: 978-0-88145-882-4

Book design: Marie Donovan
Page make-up: Adobe InDesign
Typeface: Palatino

GRATITUDE was produced by MainLine Theatre (Amy Blackmore, Artistic Director) in association with Hyper-Allergenic Productions in Montreal, Quebec, opening on 21 November 2018. The cast and creative contributors were as follows:

NAJAF (NILOUFAR) .... Michaela Di Cesare
DREW .... Patrick Keeler
JOSH .... Laurent Pitre
BEN .... Patrick Émmanuel Abellard

Co-directors .... Oren Safdie & Amy Blackmore
Set & Costume design .... Bruno-Pierre Houle
Choreography .... Amy Blackmore
Assistant stage manager .... Caitlin Helligmann
Stage manager .... Gabriel Mandeville
Publicist .... Janis Kirshner

ACKNOWLEDGEMENTS

Thank you to the Pacific Resident Theatre in Venice, California for developing the play. MainLine Theatre in Montreal for producing it. Guy Sprung and Infinithéâtre in Montreal for their continued support. And thank you to the Québec Government Office in New York & London, the Holiday Inn—Coral Gables, Florida, the Westmount Public Library, California School of the Arts in Duarte, Susan Gurman, Beth Hawk, Paul Almond, MJ Kang, Fritz Michel, Nina Safdie, Gabriel Safdie and Shelagh McFadden.

CHARACTERS & SETTING

NILOUFAR, *15, female, Middle Eastern or Indian, pretty, restless*
DREW, *16, male, class stud, failed a grade*
JOSH, *15, male, hopeless romantic, nerd, book smart*
BEN, *15, male, middle of the road, goes along with the crowd*

A shower room of a boy's locker room at a coed private high-school in Montreal

Time: The present

AUTHOR'S NOTE

Due to the ages of the characters, there should be no nudity. All simulated sex acts should be concealed by blocking, use of shower curtains, or other stage devices. It is recommended that actors be cast who are 18+ years old.

NOTE ON MUSIC

For performance of copyrighted songs, arrangements or recordings referenced in this play, permission of the copyright owner(s) must be obtained. Other songs, arrangements or recordings may be substituted provided permission from the copyright owner(s) of such songs, arrangements or recordings is obtained or songs, arrangements or recordings in the public domain may be substituted.

To the Class of 1982
St George's School of Montreal

Prologue

*(*NILOUFAR *enters, dressed in a light jacket, rolling a small suitcase. She stops at the edge of the stage— [the street curb] —and looks out, waiting. She checks her watch, looks around to see if anyone is watching her, and continues to wait…)*

(Fade to black)

Scene 1

(The shower room of a boy's locker room in a private high school in Montreal.)

*(*DREW *enters,* NILOUFAR *is right behind…)*

DREW: Come on in…

NILOUFAR: Are you sure it's okay?

DREW: Nobody uses them.

NILOUFAR: It smells like sweat or something.

DREW: That's just what boys' locker rooms smell like.

NILOUFAR: And you're sure nobody will come in?

DREW: Positive.

*(*NILOUFAR *takes out a small piece of paper from her pocket, unwraps it, and hands it to* DREW.*)*

NILOUFAR: Here…

DREW: So those are the answers?

NILOUFAR: Yes.

DREW: Because what if she changes the test?

NILOUFAR: I don't think she's going to do that.

DREW: Why not?

NILOUFAR: Well, she's pregnant. That's extra work. Doesn't seem like someone about to have a baby is going to go to the trouble when they have so many other things to worry about.

DREW: But she could change the order of the questions—I've seen other teachers do that.

NILOUFAR: I guess that can happen, but she doesn't seem like she's that clued in. During the test, she left the classroom unattended twice, probably to pee.

DREW: And it's all multiple choice?

NILOUFAR: Except the last question—but that's a bonus question.

DREW: What is it?

NILOUFAR: I wrote it down…
(She unwraps another small piece of paper.)
"Explain the general functions of D N A and R N A."

DREW: Forget it.

NILOUFAR: Do you want me to help you—

DREW: Not necessary… So you did good on the last test?

NILOUFAR: B-minus… But these aren't my answers. I mean they are, but I checked them with Karen—she was a row ahead of me.

DREW: That girl's a whiz.

NILOUFAR: I don't think she even studies.

DREW: Thanks for checking it.

NILOUFAR: Just want to make sure you'll do well.

DREW: Thanks…
(Looking at the paper)
Oh, and is that a B or a D?

NILOUFAR: D. My pen was kind of leaky—I chew my ends, bad habit.

DREW: What time is it?

NILOUFAR: You got fifteen more minutes.

DREW: I don't think I can memorize all these in time.

NILOUFAR: Why don't you write it on the back of your hand?

DREW: Never a good idea.

NILOUFAR: Why not?

DREW: I think that's where that term "getting caught red-handed" comes from.

NILOUFAR: What about your palm? Nobody will be able to see.

DREW: Then you're always opening your hand—looks really suspicious. Plus, what happens if your hands start to sweat and it smudges? …I think I'll use the inside of my shoe. Cross my leg and the whole thing's right in front of your nose.
(Showing one of his soles)
See, this was from the trig test last week.

NILOUFAR: How'd you do?

DREW: C+…I do any better and they start getting suspicious.

NILOUFAR: That's kind of funny.

DREW: Why's that funny?

NILOUFAR: I don't know—shows you don't take this whole thing too seriously.

DREW: School's a bit of a joke, isn't it?

NILOUFAR: A lot of it is useless.

DREW: I hear you.

(Pause)

NILOUFAR: You still going out with Jamie?

DREW: Me? Yeah.

NILOUFAR: That's a long time.

DREW: Almost four months.

NILOUFAR: That sounds like ages. Don't you get tired of each other?

DREW: Sometimes.

NILOUFAR: You can get other girls if you wanted. I know that for a fact.

DREW: Like who?

NILOUFAR: I don't know.

DREW: You?

NILOUFAR: Maybe… If you played your cards right.

DREW: Really?

NILOUFAR: Only if you were really, really nice to me.

DREW: Well, that's good to know, but I'm not.

NILOUFAR: What?

DREW: Very nice.

*(*NILOUFAR *laughs, taking it as a joke.)*

DREW: Well, thanks for the answers.

NILOUFAR: It was nothing.

DREW: Definitely something. What do I owe you?
(Reaching into his pocket.)
Is ten bucks all right?

NILOUFAR: You don't have to pay me anything.

DREW: No, I insist.
(Holding it out to her)
Take it.

NILOUFAR: I did it because I just wanted to—isn't that allowed anymore?

DREW: Thanks.

NILOUFAR: But it's just this one time because I don't usually cheat—

DREW: Of course.

NILOUFAR: Unless, of course, you're really in trouble with another class.

DREW: Kind of failing chemistry—but we're in the same class.

NILOUFAR: I can always help you study.

DREW: I'm not very good at that.

NILOUFAR: It's not as hard as it seems. Sometimes I think that half the battle is getting over the fact that you think you can't do something, 'cause once you actually do it, you kind of wonder what all the fear was about.

DREW: I'll try and remember that.

NILOUFAR: Like me talking to you—I was kind of intimidated for the longest time.

DREW: Really? Why?

NILOUFAR: I don't know: you're kind of considered like the class stud.

DREW: No.

NILOUFAR: Come on, you know you are…handsome, mature, confident—not like most of the boys in our class. But once we started talking it wasn't really that scary anymore.

DREW: Hey, I'm just a guy.

NILOUFAR: Exactly. And I'm just a girl.

(Awkward pause)

DREW: So I better get going—

NILOUFAR: *(With some urgency)* Maybe we can fool around… If you like.

DREW: I got class—and a girlfriend.

NILOUFAR: Right, I forgot, sorry.

DREW: Not that I don't appreciate the offer.

NILOUFAR: So I guess that means you two are exclusive to each other.

DREW: Well, we never really talked about it … But I did give her my school jacket, so that kind of implies something.

NILOUFAR: I noticed that but I didn't know that's what that meant.

DREW: Kind of, yeah. Old fashioned crap, but it still holds up.

NILOUFAR: Well, if you two ever break up, you know where to find me.

DREW: I do. And thanks again for the answers.

NILOUFAR: You're welcome … And just so you know, I make a really good girlfriend.

DREW: I'm sure.

NILOUFAR: I mean I do things—well, I don't want to brag—but guys in the past I went out with were really happy with me.

DREW: You've dated a lot of guys?

NILOUFAR: Not that many, but enough to know what I'm doing.

(She coyly unbuttons the top button on her blouse.)
Want a free sample before you go?

DREW: I can't—not that I don't want to…

NILOUFAR: You don't trust yourself.

DREW: It's kind of cheating.

NILOUFAR: Not if you accidentally bump into me and your hand accidentally slips into my…
(She slides her hand inside her blouse, over her breast.)

DREW: You don't take no for an answer.

NILOUFAR: I like you…

DREW: *(Starting to leave)* Probably just a crush—it will fade quickly, I guarantee.

NILOUFAR: *(More urgency; kind of blocking him) No.* I like you a lot.

DREW: Really.

NILOUFAR: Yes.

DREW: And what would you be willing to do to prove how much you like me?

NILOUFAR: Didn't I already do something?

DREW: Yeah, but something else. Bigger. To prove that you *really* like me.

NILOUFAR: You mean like a dare?

DREW: Kind of, but also—at the same time—a personal favor… Interested?

NILOUFAR: Depends on what it is—

DREW: Forget it.

NILOUFAR: No, no, okay, I'll do it, whatever it is… But if I do it, will you then do something for me in return?

DREW: I'll take it into consideration.

NILOUFAR: Meaning?

DREW: I'll definitely show my gratitude.

(DREW and NILOUFAR smile enticingly at each other.)

NILOUFAR: Okay…

DREW: Okay…

NILOUFAR: Okay…

(Black out)

Scene 2

(NILOUFAR and JOSH stand awkwardly near each other in the shower. After a few seconds…)

NILOUFAR: What would you like to do?

JOSH: I don't know…

NILOUFAR: It's your time.

JOSH: Drew said you would go to second base.

NILOUFAR: What does that mean?

JOSH: You know…feel you…
(Gesturing to her crotch)
Down there.

NILOUFAR: Let me see your nails?
(Checks them out)
Too long.

JOSH: I can cut them.

NILOUFAR: Do you have clippers? I'm sensitive right now.

JOSH: No, but I can trim them with my teeth.

NILOUFAR: Leaves edges… You're wasting your time. How about feeling my breast?

JOSH: Sure… Which one?

NILOUFAR: My right one's a little bigger.

*(*JOSH *comes close and feels* NILOUFAR*'s breast—almost as if it's a clinical experiment.)*

NILOUFAR: How's that?

JOSH: You're not wearing a bra.

NILOUFAR: I thought it'd be easier for you.

JOSH: I know how to undo bras. Both from the front and back.

NILOUFAR: I'm sure you do… You can go under my shirt too if you want.

JOSH: I was going to do that in a few minutes.

NILOUFAR: Up to you—it's your time…

JOSH: Does it feel good for you?

NILOUFAR: It's okay.

JOSH: Not too hard?

NILOUFAR: It's fine… You can go a little harder if you want…and kiss me too—if you want.

JOSH: Really?

NILOUFAR: Why not? While we're here.

JOSH: I just thought you like Drew—

NILOUFAR: I do, but he doesn't own me. He has a girlfriend.

JOSH: But that's why you're doing this, right? As a favor to him? And no other reason?

NILOUFAR: Kind of…I have a boyfriend too, just so you know.

JOSH: I didn't know that.

NILOUFAR: He's five years older. Studies Commerce at Concordia University. Wants to marry me after I graduate.

JOSH: Sounds serious.

NILOUFAR: It's kind of an arranged thing. Our parents know each other. His parents think I'd do well in their head-hunting business... But I can do whatever I want.

JOSH: So, are you mad at him for something?

NILOUFAR: No. Why?

JOSH: I don't know—just a thought.

NILOUFAR: Don't think so much.

JOSH: Sorry.

NILOUFAR: Aren't you excited to be here with me?

JOSH: Of course.

NILOUFAR: You're not acting like it.

JOSH: No, I am.

NILOUFAR: *(With a smile)* Are you...hard right now?

JOSH: Absolutely.

NILOUFAR: Then have some fun.

JOSH: Okay.

NILOUFAR: And if you really want to go to second base, you can do it over my underwear.

JOSH: You mean—

NILOUFAR: Just rub me. My clitoris. It's—

JOSH: I know.

(He approaches but looks a little uncertain how to proceed.)

NILOUFAR: Here, give me your hand.

*(*NILOUFAR *takes* JOSH*'s hand and slides it under her skirt.)*

NILOUFAR: You sure you know where it is?

JOSH: Yes.

NILOUFAR: Because it's a little different for every girl.

JOSH: Yeah, I know.

(He tries to locate it.)

NILOUFAR: Higher... You passed it. Lower... Stop... Not so hard... Gentler... Good... Now kiss me.

(JOSH's about to kiss NILOUFAR, but pulls away when her eyes start to close.)

NILOUFAR: What's wrong?

JOSH: Nothing.

NILOUFAR: Do I have bad breath?

JOSH: No.

NILOUFAR: Because I had garlic last night—this isn't my normal breath.

JOSH: Why did you close your eyes?

NILOUFAR: When?

JOSH: Now—when I was about to kiss you.

NILOUFAR: Just because.

JOSH: Were you pretending I'm Drew?

NILOUFAR: Not really.

JOSH: Then why did you close your eyes?

NILOUFAR: I don't know—it's what you do when you kiss. To get more into the moment.

JOSH: If you close your eyes, you could be kissing anyone.

NILOUFAR: You're the only one here.

JOSH: But if Drew were here, you'd want to kiss him more.

NILOUFAR: *(Frustrated with him)* What do you want me to say?

JOSH: I don't know.

NILOUFAR: Don't you think I'm pretty?

JOSH: Of course.

NILOUFAR: And what about my body? Isn't it sexy enough for you?

JOSH: It's absolutely magnificent.

NILOUFAR: Do you know how many guys in our grade would die to be doing what you're doing right now?

JOSH: All of them.

NILOUFAR: So why are you complicating things?

JOSH: I just want to know if you weren't doing this for Drew, would you still kind of want to be doing this with me?

NILOUFAR: Sure.

JOSH: Really?

NILOUFAR: Why not.

JOSH: But why?

NILOUFAR: I don't know... You're like one of the smartest boys in our grade. And you're funny.

JOSH: How am I funny?

NILOUFAR: I don't know... Like in Canadian History—when we had our oral presentations and you did that Louis Riel stand-up thingy.

JOSH: I made the whole accent up; I don't really know what he sounded like. I mean how could I? It was way before tape-recorders.

NILOUFAR: It was funny. Everyone laughed—even Monsieur Vailancourt—and he never smiles at anything.

JOSH: I heard his daughter was killed during a hold up at a *depanneur* a few years ago.

NILOUFAR: That's really sad... But I still hate that class. It's boring. Memorizing all those treaties: I still have no idea what they're for.

JOSH: To avoid wars.

NILOUFAR: At least wars make interesting history.

JOSH: Maybe they should throw in a little history of the United States.

NILOUFAR: *(With a chuckle)* See, that's funny!

*(*JOSH *and* NILOUFAR *look at each other and connect. He moves in to kiss her.)*

*(*BEN *enters.)*

BEN: Hey.

*(*JOSH *and* NILOUFAR *break away from each other.)*

BEN: Sorry, there was nothing to knock on.

JOSH: What are you doing here?

BEN: Drew sent me.

JOSH: What does he want?

BEN: Nothing. He just said, well, I can be here too.

JOSH: To watch?

BEN: No…

JOSH: Then what?

BEN: You know, do things with Nilou.

*(*JOSH *looks to* NILOUFAR.*)*

JOSH: Do you know anything about this?

NILOUFAR: I don't know, he said a friend or two…

JOSH: A friend or *two*?

NILOUFAR: I don't remember.

JOSH: No restrictions. Just anyone. Maybe Floyd Kessler?

NILOUFAR: No, definitely not Floyd; he has way too much acne.

JOSH: But if Drew sent him?

NILOUFAR: He wouldn't.

BEN: I'm not quite sure what's going on here but—

JOSH: Shut up.

BEN: Look, I got class in fifteen minutes and Drew said—

NILOUFAR: It's fine—you can stay.

JOSH: Well, I'm not leaving.

NILOUFAR: Do whatever you want.
(To BEN*)*
You want to feel my breast, Ben?

BEN: Sure.
(He starts to move in.)

JOSH: *(Moving in to claim his breast)* Hey, hey! That's *my* side.

BEN: Either one's okay with me.

JOSH: That one's smaller.

BEN: I don't care.

*(*BEN *and* JOSH *both move in and feel one breast.)*

NILOUFAR: *(To both of them)* Hey, I'm not a cow. Go easy.

BEN: Sorry.

NILOUFAR: That's better.

BEN: You have no bra on.

JOSH: You're so observant.

NILOUFAR: You can feel under my shirt.

BEN: Can I finger you?

JOSH: She just said you could feel under her shirt.

BEN: I got to go in five minutes and Drew said second base.

NILOUFAR: Let me see your nails.

JOSH: You're going to let him?

(BEN shows NILOUFAR his nails.)

NILOUFAR: Okay, but be gentle—it's sensitive—I'm getting my period soon.

BEN: But not today.

NILOUFAR: No.

JOSH: *(To NILOUFAR)* What are you doing?

NILOUFAR: I have to be fair.

JOSH: To who?

NILOUFAR: *(To BEN)* Not so rough.

BEN: Oh my God, it's like wet.

JOSH: I'm responsible for that.

BEN: But that's not pee.

NILOUFAR: Of course not.

BEN: Can I kiss you?

NILOUFAR: Sure.

JOSH: I'm not going to kiss you after you kiss him.

NILOUFAR: You had your chance.

(BEN and NILOUFAR kiss.)

JOSH: Okay stop! …Stop!!!

(They stop kissing.)

JOSH: There's a reason why Drew told me to be here before you—he wanted me to be with her first.

BEN: That's bull shit. I just got let out of French class late.

JOSH: This is wrong.

BEN: Then leave.

JOSH: Can't you just wait outside for a few minutes—

BEN: I got class soon.

NILOUFAR: Me too.

JOSH: Maybe you two can meet up somewhere tomorrow.

NILOUFAR: No way; the deal is only for this one time.

BEN: We could flip a coin.

NILOUFAR: Can we just get it over with and do this?

JOSH: There are obviously a few complications.

NILOUFAR: I'll give you both hand jobs.

*(*BEN *and* JOSH *look at each other with surprise.)*

JOSH: What?

BEN: Cool.

JOSH: You mean at the same time?

NILOUFAR: *(Directing traffic)* Just come over to this side and you stay over on that side.

JOSH: I do not want to see his dick.

NILOUFAR: Just look the other away—you won't even know he's here.

*(*BEN *and* JOSH *move in.)*

NILOUFAR: Undo your own pants—I only have two hands.

*(*BEN *and* JOSH *undo their pants and* NILOUFAR *slides her hands into their respective pants. There's an audible groan of pleasure from both of them.)*

NILOUFAR: Happy now?

*(*NILOUFAR *starts jerking* BEN *and* JOSH *off.)*

BEN: Oh my God…

JOSH: Quiet.

BEN: Ohhhh.

JOSH: Shut up!

NILOUFAR: Tell me before you're going to—

BEN: Ugh!!!

*(*BEN *has an orgasm and* NILOUFAR *pushes both* BEN *and* JOSH *away. They quickly cover up.)*

NILOUFAR: Fuck! You got it all over my skirt.

BEN: Sorry.

JOSH: What's your problem?

BEN: *(Panicked; starting to leave)* Nothing…I don't know…I got to get to class.

NILOUFAR: Do you have any money?

BEN: For what?

JOSH: Look what you did to her dress.

BEN: Money wasn't part of the deal. Nobody said anything about paying money.

NILOUFAR: I'm saying it now.

BEN: That changes everything, makes it into a prostitute thing, and I have a policy of never paying for it.

JOSH: She's going to have to take that to the cleaners.

NILOUFAR: Yeah.

BEN: I know for a fact that cum comes out in the regular wash.

JOSH: Give her five bucks.

BEN: No way… Anyway, I got to get to class. Thanks. *(He runs out.)*

NILOUFAR: *(Looking at her skirt)* I can't go to class like this.

*(*JOSH *comes over to* NILOUFAR *and pulls a couple of tissues from his pocket.)*

JOSH: Here's some Kleenex.

*(*NILOUFAR *takes it and tries to rub it out.)*

NILOUFAR: It's only making it worse.

JOSH: Maybe with some water.

*(*JOSH *tries to open the shower faucet but nothing comes out. He tries the next one but all that happens is the pipe shakes.)*

NILOUFAR: Forget it.

JOSH: It's almost time for class.

NILOUFAR: I'm not leaving until it dries.

JOSH: You want me to wait with you?

NILOUFAR: No point both of us missing class.

JOSH: I don't mind.

NILOUFAR: Do whatever you want… But I'm not doing anything more.

JOSH: That's fine.

*(*JOSH *and* NILOUFAR *sit on the floor… The bell rings in the distance.)*

NILOUFAR: You can leave; I'm okay on my own.

*(*JOSH *just sits.)*

NILOUFAR: I don't need you, Josh.

*(*JOSH *just sits. After a moment…)*

JOSH: So what do you think of Ben?

NILOUFAR: He's pretty dumb.

JOSH: Yeah, that's Ben.

NILOUFAR: Are you guys friends?

JOSH: Well, he's friends with Drew and I'm friends with Drew, but if we weren't friends with Drew I don't think we'd even talk.

NILOUFAR: ...You're bigger than him.

JOSH: Actually he's half an inch taller—he just has bad posture. Drew calls him Caveman.

NILOUFAR: No. You're "bigger" than him. Your penis.

JOSH: Oh... What about compared to your boyfriend?

NILOUFAR: ...I don't know.

JOSH: You mean you haven't done it with him?

NILOUFAR: It's a different kind of thing. Our parents know each other. Our families originate from the same small village. There are customs that need to be followed ... But I get to make the final decision.

JOSH: Lucky.

NILOUFAR: Not really.

JOSH: So then this was the first time you—

NILOUFAR: Not with the kissing, not with feeling, kind of the first time with the fingering, and definitely the first time touching a guy's penis.

JOSH: Me too...with a girl touching my penis...and the touching over the underwear.

NILOUFAR: What about breasts?

JOSH: No, I've done that twice.

NILOUFAR: With who?

JOSH: Joelle. At Barry's party.

NILOUFAR: What about Mike?

JOSH: He wasn't there. He lives far away. I think he even has to take a train to school.

NILOUFAR: Does he know?

JOSH: I don't think so.

NILOUFAR: Oh, he really loves her.

JOSH: Yeah, I know. I feel bad. But we were both a little drunk.

NILOUFAR: That's no excuse…

JOSH: No, it isn't. But I could have gone further if I wanted.

NILOUFAR: That was good of you not to.

JOSH: I guess.

NILOUFAR: She probably likes you then.

JOSH: Maybe.

NILOUFAR: But you don't like her.

JOSH: I kind of like her, but she's so quiet.

NILOUFAR: She looks a little boyish.

JOSH: That too… She should really grow out her hair.

NILOUFAR: And the other time?

JOSH: Oh, well… Just now.

NILOUFAR: So that's really once.

JOSH: Yeah.

NILOUFAR: You're still young.

JOSH: Drew's only a year older.

NILOUFAR: I know… But he drives.

JOSH: Is that important?

NILOUFAR: Yes…

JOSH: Would you let him go all the way?

NILOUFAR: Probably.

JOSH: And if your boyfriend tried?

NILOUFAR: Oh, he wouldn't.

JOSH: Can I kiss you now?

NILOUFAR: I'm kind of not in the mood anymore.

(JOSH *is disappointed.)*

NILOUFAR: All right, one short kiss and then we're back to being friends.

JOSH: We were never friends.

NILOUFAR: Then we can become friends.

JOSH: Won't it be weird?

NILOUFAR: Why?

JOSH: You touched me. I felt you.

NILOUFAR: So what, it's just body parts... Now kiss me.

(JOSH *approaches* NILOUFAR *and starts to kiss her. She breaks it off the second it starts getting intimate.)*

NILOUFAR: *(Regarding the stain on her dress)* I think it's almost dry.

JOSH: We've only missed a few minutes of class.

NILOUFAR: Maybe they won't notice if we sneak in.

JOSH: I'll go first and make sure nobody's in the locker room.

NILOUFAR: That would be great.

(JOSH *exits.)*

(NILOUFAR *checks the stain, tussles her hair, fixes her clothes.)*

JOSH: *(V O)* Coast is clear!

(NILOUFAR *exits as lights...)*

(Fade to black)

Scene 3

*(*NILOUFAR *is waiting in the shower room as* DREW *enters.)*

DREW: Sorry I'm late—I had to drive Jamie to her dance class.

NILOUFAR: Does she take ballet?

DREW: Modern Jazz—whatever that is.

NILOUFAR: She's lucky to have you to drive her.

DREW: Sometimes I think she takes advantage. Were you waiting long?

NILOUFAR: Only fifteen minutes.

DREW: Sorry—not sure why we had to meet today.

NILOUFAR: We said we would.

DREW: You want to go outside? It's stopped raining.

NILOUFAR: Here's fine.

DREW: 'Cause it's really starting to stink down here.

NILOUFAR: I like it; it's more private.

DREW: Suit yourself. What's up?

NILOUFAR: I did what you asked.

DREW: Yeah, I heard from Josh and Ben. I think you made their lives.

NILOUFAR: I wanted you to be happy.

DREW: I'm happy you made them happy.

NILOUFAR: Good.

DREW: Thanks.
(Pause)
Is there anything else you wanted to talk about?

NILOUFAR: It's just I did what you asked.

DREW: Yeah, I know, thanks.

NILOUFAR: You're welcome.

DREW: So?

NILOUFAR: Oh, come on!

DREW: What?

NILOUFAR: You know what; I did what you asked.

DREW: Look, you did a wonderful thing for two desperate guys in need.

NILOUFAR: I jerked off two of your loser friends.

DREW: Let's not make this personal.

NILOUFAR: They put their sweaty hands all over my body.

DREW: You must've enjoyed it somewhat… I mean, just a little?

NILOUFAR: You said—

DREW: I'd take it into consideration.

NILOUFAR: And show your gratitude. That was the word you used. You said the word gratitude.

DREW: And I am very grateful to you, Nilou.

NILOUFAR: No, gratitude means more than that. Showing gratitude means you do something for someone who's done something for you.

DREW: What do you want me to do?

NILOUFAR: You know what.

DREW: I can't do that.

NILOUFAR: You said you couldn't do it, but if I did something for you—

DREW: Okay, we're going in circles here. You know I have a girlfriend.

NILOUFAR: *(Starting to cry)* Why are you doing this to me?

DREW: I'm not doing anything to you.

NILOUFAR: It was understood…

DREW: Maybe by you, but not by me.

NILOUFAR: She doesn't have to know.

DREW: *I'll* know.

NILOUFAR: You owe me this.

DREW: You knew I have a girlfriend.

NILOUFAR: Why can't we just try fooling around a bit, and if you don't like it—

DREW: No.

NILOUFAR: *(Putting her arm out)* Feel my skin; it's really soft.

DREW: No.

NILOUFAR: 'Cause I know that once you get to know me—

DREW: I know you fine. We have two classes together.

NILOUFAR: But that's not who I really am—

DREW: Then stop pretending to be someone you're not.

NILOUFAR: That's what I'm doing right now.

DREW: Look, I got to go.

NILOUFAR: *(She grabs his arm—getting in his face.)* I can do things for you that Jamie won't.

DREW: Let go of my arm.

NILOUFAR: I promise I won't tell her.

DREW: It's how *I* feel, not her.

*(*NILOUFAR *slides* DREW*'s hand over her breast. He jerks it away and holds her firmly by both arms.)*

DREW: *(Trying to get through to her)* I love Jamie!

NILOUFAR: No you don't. You like that she's popular, that she's perky and giggly and fun. But I see the way you look at her, and that's not the way someone looks at someone when they're in love. She's like a trophy that you won, and you love watching everyone else looking at you, admiring you for winning her over. But Jamie is not who you really want.

*(*DREW *is upended for a brief moment, as what* NILOUFAR *is saying hits a mark.)*

DREW: You don't know what you're talking about.

*(*NILOUFAR *senses* DREW*'s hesitation.)*

NILOUFAR: I think I do. You want to be free.
(Approaching again)
...Let me help you. I'll let you do anything you want...

DREW: No.

NILOUFAR: I think your nos mean yes.

DREW: Stop it.

NILOUFAR: Come on, I just want to be with you... For a minute, I swear. I won't tell Jamie. It will be our secret. I love you.

DREW: *(Pushing her away)* What the fuck do you love about me? Huh? My looks? My hair? My chin? My body? Do you also love that I failed a grade? Or that I'm barely passing this year?

NILOUFAR: You'll pass—I'll help you.

DREW: Do you know what that means? Nobody fails two grades.

NILOUFAR: You're street smart not book smart, that's all.

DREW: Come on, Nilou—I've smoked so much weed since I was thirteen, I can barely remember my phone number.

NILOUFAR: I don't care. You're sensitive and wise... kind.

DREW: Do you understand what I just did to you?

NILOUFAR: I take full responsibility. I wanted to do it for you. If it made you happy, it made me happy. That's the kind of person I am. And to tell you the truth, it was probably good for me .

DREW: That is so pathetic!

NILOUFAR: I know you don't mean that.

DREW: What are you, a fucking moron?

NILOUFAR: You're feeling vulnerable right now, scared of what this could turn into, but I promise—

DREW: Get it into your head, Nilou! There is no fucking way in hell that I would lay two fingers on you let alone go out with you. You're a fucking freak of nature and— ...And I'm out of here.

*(*NILOUFAR *falls to the floor and grabs* DREW*'s leg.)*

NILOUFAR: You're not leaving!

DREW: Let go of my leg.

*(*DREW *kicks* NILOUFAR *off and starts to exit.)*

NILOUFAR: You walk out of here, and I'm going straight to Principal Wallace!!

DREW: Oooo. And what are you going to say?

NILOUFAR: I'll tell him what Josh and Ben did to me.

DREW: What *they* did to *you*?

NILOUFAR: *(Not completely sure where this line of attack will lead)* How they forced me to do things to them.

DREW: Oh, yeah, right, twisted your arm, put a gun to your head, and took you down into the shower room.

NILOUFAR: I have all the proof I need... Just like Monica Lewinsky—

DREW: Who?

NILOUFAR: Don't you know your history? The blue dress. President Clinton's sperm ... I have Ben's all over my skirt.

DREW: That's bull shit.

NILOUFAR: Not to mention there were two of them. Easy to see how I couldn't just run away... You better believe they'll believe me.

DREW: Fine, but I had nothing to do with that.

NILOUFAR: You don't think your name will come up?

DREW: You can't be serious.

(NILOUFAR lets out a scream.)

DREW: Would you shut the fuck up!

NILOUFAR: I swear I'll tell them everything; how you told me to meet you here, how instead I was met by your friends, how they grabbed me—

DREW: Nilou—

NILOUFAR: Held me down, taking turns raping me—

DREW: Rape?

NILOUFAR: If you think you can trick me into being with your friends and not hold up your end of what was agreed upon—

DREW: Okay, okay, relax—I hear you.

NILOUFAR: I'm not playing around here!

DREW: Okay.

NILOUFAR: I will not be made a fool of.

DREW: We'll work it out—just calm down.

NILOUFAR: I want to know *how* we're going to work it out.

DREW: *(Panicked; exasperated)* What the hell do you want from me?

NILOUFAR: I did something for you…

DREW: I told you I was grateful.

NILOUFAR: Then show me gratitude…

DREW: …Okay.

NILOUFAR: Okay?

DREW: Okay.

NILOUFAR: Kiss me.

*(*DREW *hesitantly moves in towards* NILOUFAR *and gives her a kiss on the cheek.)*

NILOUFAR: On the lips—

DREW: You really want me to—

NILOUFAR: *(In control)* Like you mean it.

*(*DREW *hesitates;* NILOUFAR *moves in to kiss him while he remains as still as a statue.)*

NILOUFAR: Kiss me back… Mouth open.

*(*DREW *doesn't comply.)*

*(*NILOUFAR *lets out another scream.* DREW *quickly goes to kiss her, aggressively cutting off her scream. She willfully takes this for passion.)*

NILOUFAR: Feel me…

*(*DREW *doesn't reply.* NILOUFAR *takes his hand and slips it under her shirt. He remains still but lets her guide his hand.)*

NILOUFAR: …How do they feel?

DREW: *(Forced)* Nice.

NILOUFAR: Yeah, now feel this…

*(*NILOUFAR *starts to move* DREW*'s hand up her skirt.)*

DREW: Nilou, no.

*(*NILOUFAR *prepares to scream again. He covers her mouth.)*

DREW: Okay, okay.

*(*DREW*'s hand moves under* NILOUFAR*'s skirt and she starts to feel pleasure.)*

NILOUFAR: Do you feel that? ...That's how you make me feel... Want to make love to me?

(No response; more forceful:)

NILOUFAR: Make love to me.

DREW: I don't have protection.

NILOUFAR: *(Starts to unbutton his pants)* It's safe.

DREW: No it's not.

*(*NILOUFAR *slides her hand in* DREW*'s underwear. He reacts as if it's cold water.)*

NILOUFAR: *(Discovers he's not hard)* You're a little nervous, that's okay.
(After a few moments of trying to get him hard.)
I know what will help...

*(*NILOUFAR*'s about to go down on her knees but* DREW *stops her.)*

DREW: Stop... Stop! ...It won't work.

NILOUFAR: *(Turning rejection into a positive)* You can't cheat on her, can you?

DREW: No.

NILOUFAR: That's kind of sweet.

DREW: Not really.

NILOUFAR: You have a good heart.

DREW: I don't know.

NILOUFAR: It would probably be best if you break up with Jamie first...

DREW: Well—

NILOUFAR: It's really what you should do.

DREW: It's not that easy.

NILOUFAR: Don't worry, I don't care if it takes a little time... We'll wait.

DREW: *(Playing along)* Okay.

NILOUFAR: Okay?

DREW: Okay.

NILOUFAR: Don't worry, I'm not crazy.

DREW: I know.

NILOUFAR: I just need to know that you'll be here for me if I really need you.

DREW: I'm here for you.

*(*NILOUFAR *gives* DREW *one last kiss and exits.)*

*(*DREW *is mortified.)*

(Black out)

Scene 4

*(*NILOUFAR *is waiting anxiously in the shower room.* JOSH *enters, shell-shocked.)*

JOSH: What the fuck!

NILOUFAR: I'm sorry—

JOSH: Two bullets through my head?

NILOUFAR: I know, he's crazy.

JOSH: Obviously.

NILOUFAR: But he means it—

JOSH: Yeah, well, he sounded like he meant it. How'd he even get my number?

NILOUFAR: I don't know, but he's capable of doing these things. You have to go.

JOSH: Where am I going to go?

NILOUFAR: You're going to have to switch schools.

JOSH: What?!

NILOUFAR: You shouldn't even be here right now. It's not safe. He might be waiting outside. He has friends—they look out for each other.

JOSH: He'll go to jail.

NILOUFAR: He doesn't care about something like that right now.

JOSH: I don't understand, how did this happen?

NILOUFAR: He's smart about things like this.

JOSH: Things like what? Someone had to tell him.

NILOUFAR: He senses things—

JOSH: Because it was only me, you and Ben. Maybe Drew. But I don't think he would say anything.

NILOUFAR: No.

JOSH: Then it must be Ben—that asshole—

NILOUFAR: Ben didn't say anything.

JOSH: How do you know? The guy looks all stupid and innocent, but—

NILOUFAR: I told him.

JOSH: You told him?

NILOUFAR: Yes.

JOSH: Why?

NILOUFAR: It slipped out.

JOSH: How does something like that slip out?

NILOUFAR: By accident. I was drunk. It was our second anniversary. He took me out to this fancy seafood restaurant, and he ordered wine—which we never drink—and I got really drunk. And then, I don't remember, I passed out.

JOSH: So how do you know you said anything?

NILOUFAR: When I woke up, he was yelling at me, pressing me with all these questions: "Who's Josh?" "What'd you do in the locker room with Josh?" I didn't even know what I told him and he was making all these crazy threats if I didn't tell him everything—

JOSH: But you didn't tell him everything.

NILOUFAR: No.

JOSH: Just about me.

NILOUFAR: I had to give him something—and he already knew your name.

JOSH: But I didn't even really finger you.

NILOUFAR: I had no control of what came out.

JOSH: And you didn't mention Drew's name?

NILOUFAR: No.

JOSH: Ben's? Because he's really the one you did something with—if you want to be technical about it. He's the one your boyfriend should be pissed about.

NILOUFAR: I know—

JOSH: So tell him you got the names mixed up—get Ben to switch schools. He only came in last year. I've been here since I was six—both my sister and aunt went to this school.

NILOUFAR: There's no getting through to him right now. If I say anything, he just slaps my face, and starts shaking me.

JOSH: That's abuse! Don't you know your rights? You can have him arrested for that.

NILOUFAR: I can't do that.

JOSH: Why not?

NILOUFAR: I just can't.

JOSH: Then I'll call the police—do it anonymously. Tell them I saw him slapping you around in a parking lot.

NILOUFAR: No.

JOSH: Because you know you can get a restraining order against him. Can't come within a hundred metres. My mother did that to my father once, and all he did was throw her into a cold shower.

NILOUFAR: It will only get him more angry and he'll find a way to get back at me.

JOSH: Then maybe you need to talk to your parents—have them confront his parents.

NILOUFAR: Are you crazy? If he tells my parents they'll be on his side. The whole community will find out about what I did. They'll disown me.

JOSH: I'm sure if the community finds out that he's beating you they'll—

NILOUFAR: You don't get it. This is a different world. Everybody in my neighborhood knows everybody else's business. My older sister married into a very respectable family. It's not only me that this will affect. If what I did gets out, my life is basically over.

JOSH: Yeah, I get it. I get a B on a test and it's suddenly like—

NILOUFAR: You're not hearing me. There is no other option here. I'm trying to save your life. I'm sure there are other good private schools you can go to.

JOSH: And what will stop him from finding me there?

NILOUFAR: If you leave now, he'll leave you alone and let this pass—it's in his interest too. He just can't stand the thought of us being in the same school together. It's driving him crazy.

JOSH: Then maybe it would be better if you switched schools. Something more traditional, like a Catholic school. All girls. He'll be happy with that.

NILOUFAR: That's impossible. Believe me, if I could change, I would.

JOSH: Then just do it!

NILOUFAR: My parents will ask questions, and my boyfriend will tell them everything.

JOSH: Tell *them* what he did to you.

NILOUFAR: Please, I'm begging you. I couldn't live with myself if anything happened to you.

JOSH: I know! ...I'll ask my Dad to get me a body guard.

NILOUFAR: Then the whole school will start to ask questions. My reputation will be ruined. It will get back to my community and—

JOSH: Not if—

NILOUFAR: Stop it! There's no other way!

(JOSH starts to pace back and forth, thinking of a way out.)

NILOUFAR: I'm begging you ... please.

JOSH: *(Frustrated)* Fuck!

NILOUFAR: I'm so sorry.

JOSH: This is fucking nuts!

NILOUFAR: I know... But I'll be forever grateful to you.

JOSH: *(Sarcastic)* Whoopee.

NILOUFAR: ...If you do this for me, I'll...I'll show you my gratitude...

JOSH: What the fuck does that supposed to mean?

NILOUFAR: Right now.

JOSH: Right now, what?

(NILOUFAR moves in to kiss JOSH.)

JOSH: No.

(NILOUFAR starts to get down on her knees but JOSH won't let her.)

JOSH: No way.

NILOUFAR: *(She puts her hands on him.)* Make love to me.

JOSH: Not like this.

NILOUFAR: Please...

JOSH: I—

NILOUFAR: *(Starting to undo his belt)* Let's go to fourth base...I want you in me, please.

JOSH: *(Resisting less)* But—

NILOUFAR: Stop talking.

(NILOUFAR kisses JOSH on the mouth, then manages to lower his pants, and raise her skirt, before inserting his penis in her.)

JOSH: *(The most amazing thing he's ever felt.)* Oh...my God!

NILOUFAR: You feel so good.

JOSH: I can't hold it—

NILOUFAR: Don't—

JOSH: I can't—

NILOUFAR: Stop fighting—

JOSH: I'm going to—

NILOUFAR: Let go—

JOSH: Agh!...

*(*JOSH *has an orgasm and collapses into* NILOUFAR*'s arms. After a moment, he collects himself and withdraws. He looks at her and wants to kiss her, but she pulls away.)*

NILOUFAR: You better go out the back and climb over the fence… It will be safer.

JOSH: It will take me a few days to get things together.

NILOUFAR: I'll tell him. If he knows you're really leaving, he'll leave you alone.

*(*JOSH *is about to leave, but comes back.)*

JOSH: Do you think, well, once I switch schools, we might be able to… Maybe in secret…meet with each other.

NILOUFAR: Don't come to me, I'll find you… Now, go.

*(*JOSH *exits.)*

*(*NILOUFAR *exhales with a sense of relief as lights…)*

(Fade to black)

Scene 5

*(*BEN *and* DREW *are in the shower room, sharing a small mickey of vodka—passing it back and forth.)*

DREW: Did you get to feel those tits?

BEN: Fucking hard as rock.

DREW: And those nipples.

BEN: Like erasers. I swear I was just like, pinch me. Is this really happening?

DREW: She has pretty soft skin, aye?

BEN: She has the fucking most amazing skin. It was totally awesome. Like exotic.

DREW: Who takes care of you like Drew does.

BEN: I owe you, big time.

DREW: But she didn't blow you?

BEN: No, I asked—and she wanted to—but with Josh there—

DREW: Yeah.

BEN: Did she blow you?

DREW: Oh, the fucking works.

BEN: Fuck. What was that like?

DREW: Seriously—with those lips?—Do you even have to ask?

BEN: Yeah, I do.

DREW: I don't really like to kiss and tell.

BEN: Oh, come on—at least give me the highlights.

DREW: Seriously?

BEN: Fuck, yes.

DREW: All right… Well, she has this incredible suction thing going on.

BEN: Like a straw?

DREW: More like a Hoover. And it's—well, almost like she doesn't have any back to her throat—because I ain't exactly small, you know—yet she managed to take me all in, and I'm wondering how is this even humanly possible? …Like when you watch a guy swallow swords?

BEN: Holy shit.

DREW: And then she just starts drawing my wad from the base of my dick, building it and building it, like my whole body became this volcano with molten lava bubbling inside, and I felt the pressure building from my toes, up my legs, the whole thing getting ready to explode, but I didn't 'cause she was like two steps ahead of me—knew exactly what to do, always in control, keeping me from going past the point of no return. You know that point?

BEN: Oh, yeah.

DREW: Rising and falling, rising and falling, and then just when I thought this is it, and my whole body seizes up to go ballistic … she lets go.

BEN: Oh no.

DREW: And starts the whole thing over again. And she did this like five times, until my nuts felt like they were being squeezed by a vice.

BEN: Fucking double-ouch.

DREW: And then for that last time, she just, I mean it was—I almost wished I was her if you know what I mean…

BEN: Yeah…

DREW: Can you imagine the power she felt being able to bring me to that point and then experience the explosion of my whole body in her mouth? I mean it was pretty spectacular on my end, but for her, it must've been … I don't know…

BEN: What?

DREW: It just got me thinking—not that I'd ever go fag—I mean, I love women more than anything in the world, those curvy bodies, long silky hair—

BEN: Love that—

DREW: But from a purely mechanical point of view, sucking dick is probably a lot more interesting than licking pussy, if you know what I mean.

BEN: I can kind of see that… More active.

DREW: Exactly. I mean sticking your tongue up there is fun and all, but we're constantly sticking things into them: our fingers, tongues, noses, dicks, but, on a deeper level, well, it's all kind of safe.

BEN: Safe?

DREW: Well, maybe not safe in the way a vagina could be a pretty scary place—especially around that time of the month, but safe in that, well—we're not really taking any risks. It's all outside stuff. We're not letting anything in... But a chick—stuff is penetrating her all the time: her vagina, her mouth, and that's got to feel a lot more vulnerable. And when you're vulnerable, well, that's kind of probably when you feel the most arousion.

BEN: ...I can see that.

DREW: Too bad we'll never be chicks. I mean, like for a day or something.

BEN: Yeah, that'd be a trip if we could actually just try it for a day.

DREW: Although, I suppose, in reality, we could.

BEN: I don't see how—

DREW: Well, obviously we can't just turn into chicks...

BEN: Unless you get a sex change operation.

DREW: Fuck that. But, you know, the sensation of what it might feel like? ...You can probably experience that...if you wanted.

BEN: *(Starting to feel uncomfortable)* Umm...

DREW: We can kind of experience *that*...
(He slowly gets down on his knees.)

BEN: What are you doing?

DREW: *(Jumps back to his feet)* Gotha!!!

BEN: *(Uncomfortable laugh)* What the fuck?

DREW: Kind of looked interested there for second, Benny.

BEN: No fucking way.

DREW: Oh, yeah, just a little.

BEN: You're messing with me.

DREW: Absolutely.

BEN: Very funny. Ha-ha.

DREW: Well, if not interested, definitely excited...
(Looking down at his crotch.)
I could see that... Got the big bulge going.

BEN: That's just the way my fly bunches up.

DREW: Yeah, right.

BEN: Fucking aye.

*(*BEN*'s and* DREW*'s laughing dies down... Silence)*

DREW: But if we're going to be honest with each other—like totally honest—there's definitely a part of me that wanted to know how it felt—from the other side. Like if you're a quarter back all the time, you should kind of be a receiver a couple of times, just so you know what it's like being the person you're throwing to. It makes you into a better all 'round player.

BEN: I don't know.

DREW: You mean to tell me you've never thought about it? I mean not thought about it thought about it—but, like when you're not really thinking about anything, and it just kind of slips into your mind as much as you try and fight it.

BEN: Hey, I'm not gay.

DREW: That's fucking gross. Two guys kissing? That makes me want to puke.

BEN: I hear you.

DREW: No, this won't be like that...

BEN: This...?

DREW: Come on, Benny, we're being totally honest best friends here. I could definitely see you wanted to.

BEN: No—

DREW: I mean, I kind of got turned on too, going down on my knees.

BEN: Yeah?

DREW: Definitely. It's nothing to be ashamed of.
(More uncomfortable silence)
So, what if we tried it—just this one time—

BEN: I don't know—

DREW: Nobody would ever have to know.

BEN: *(Starts to leave)* I think I better get to class—

DREW: *(Blocking him)* Hold on. Just play this out. Let's see what it feels like. We can always stop. Think of it as an experiment—like we're in Mr Siddiqui's Chemistry Class.

BEN: *(Trying to deflect; in an Indian accent)* "Kitchen Curry" —I love the way he says that.

*(*DREW *slowly reaches down and carefully unzips* BEN*'s pants and then puts his hand in the slot.)*

*(*BEN *reacts with a wince.)*

DREW: Is that so bad?

BEN: What if someone—

DREW: Nobody's coming in here.

BEN: I've changed my mind.

DREW: Relax... Just close your eyes and imagine I'm Nilou—with that tan skin, and those thick lips.

*(*BEN *closes his eyes.)*

DREW: Or maybe I'm even Jamie…I'll show you what she does to me, with those long legs, little blond hairs on her thigh, leading up to her…

*(*DREW *gets down on his knees and starts giving* BEN *a blow job.)*

*(*JOSH *enters, sees them, is in shock, and exits before either of them see him.)*

*(*BEN *has an orgasm.)*

BEN: Sorry.

(Feeling extremely uncomfortable, BEN *quickly zips up his pants and prepares to leave but* DREW *kind of blocks his way.)*

DREW: That was pretty cool.

BEN: *(Unenthusiastically)* Yeah?

DREW: Cool as shit. Doesn't taste as bad as I thought—in fact it kind of tasted good. Kind of like dill pickles. Did you eat anything like that last night?

BEN: Just chicken and French Fries.

DREW: I had pineapple—fruit's supposed to make it sweeter. Want to see if it works?

BEN: Maybe tomorrow.

DREW: Because, I swear, I suddenly feel like I have this totally different perspective on chicks.

BEN: That's great.

(Trying to pass but being blocked.)

BEN: Can I get by please?

DREW: Come on, Benny…I did it for you.

BEN: I'm just feeling a little dizzy right now.

DREW: And you do kind of owe me.

BEN: For what?

DREW: Don't think that whole set-up with Nilou didn't cost me.

BEN: I told you, I really appreciated it.

DREW: So?

BEN: I just don't think I can go through with this.

DREW: How do you know if you don't try?

BEN: *(Snapping)* I just do, all right!

DREW: *(Hitting back)* Don't fucking get testy with me! Do you know what I had to do to protect you?

BEN: Protect me from what?

DREW: The fucking bitch threatened to report you for rape?

*(*BEN *looks surprised.)*

DREW: Oh, you're surprised? Shoot your load with all that D N A all over her skirt and expect that shit ain't going to come back at you?

BEN: But she did it to me.

DREW: You are so fucking naive. Don't you know anything about women? ...Monica Drabinsky?

BEN: Who?

DREW: Because of you, I was forced to fuck that skanky ass bitch—risk losing the most precious thing to me so that you wouldn't be kicked out of this school and locked up in the slammer for the next twenty years. And if that's not enough, you just tricked me into sucking your dick! ...I don't think it's asking too much for you to get down on your knees and reciprocate...

*(*BEN *realizes he has no choice, but is also incredibly uncomfortable and unable to proceed. He looks down at* DREW*'s crotch, starts to go down on his knees, but rises back*

up. DREW *puts his hands on* BEN*'s shoulders and gently—but forcefully—pushes him down.)*

DREW: You'll see… Your whole perspective on chicks will change after this…I guarantee it.

(Fade to black)

Scene 6

(The shower room. JOSH waits anxiously. NILOUFAR finally enters.

JOSH: I know-I know…

NILOUFAR: You're not supposed to be here anymore—

JOSH: I'm still considering leaving but—

NILOUFAR: Considering? You promised.

JOSH: I know.

NILOUFAR: You can't just change your mind.

JOSH: I haven't—completely.

NILOUFAR: What does that mean?

JOSH: Just hear me out—

NILOUFAR: He's got his friends following me—

JOSH: The guy with the mustache in the minivan? Don't worry—I saw him across the street.

NILOUFAR: Did he see you?

JOSH: I'm pretty sure not.

NILOUFAR: Oh my God.

JOSH: Just hear me out.

NILOUFAR: Why are you doing this to me?

JOSH: I think I've come up with a better plan.

NILOUFAR: There's no changing his mind. I told him you were leaving, and he agreed to leave you alone—he calmed down. He said he'd accept that. But if he finds out you're still here, he'll think I'm lying—

JOSH: I was very careful, I promise. Please hear me out for a second—

NILOUFAR: Because he's not stupid.

JOSH: I wore this.

Josh shows her a hat and sunglasses.

NILOUFAR: I can't believe this is happening.

JOSH: Just let me—

NILOUFAR: You're sure nobody followed you?

JOSH: Yeah…pretty sure—

NILOUFAR: Pretty sure? These guys are like trained professionally.

JOSH: Niloufar—that's your full name, isn't it?

NILOUFAR: *(Pushing him out)* You have to leave!

JOSH: *(Stopping)* I think you really want me to stay.

NILOUFAR: What? Why are you—I just asked you to go.

JOSH: Yes, I understand that.

NILOUFAR: Do you have a problem with your hearing?

JOSH: No. But everything you've done tells me that you really want me to stay—maybe not at this school, but I think you want me to stay…in your life.

NILOUFAR: You're talking crazy.

JOSH: Okay, maybe I'm a little tired—I haven't slept in three nights—and as you can imagine my family's a little suspicious why I want to switch schools in the middle of the year after being here for eleven years—actually, they think it's because I'm being bullied—but once I broke down and told my mother the truth—

NILOUFAR: You told your mother?!

JOSH: Don't worry, I made her swear not to tell anybody, and she's really good with her word.

NILOUFAR: What'd you tell her?

JOSH: Pretty much everything—

NILOUFAR: Oh my God.

JOSH: Leaving out certain details, of course, sexual and— ...The thing is she was really helpful putting things in perspective.

NILOUFAR: I'm going to be sick.

JOSH: See, when she was our age, she met my father who completely fell in love with *her*—even though he sort of had a girlfriend—which made her suspicious, which later proved valid—but at the time, she didn't know he would turn into a cheater. She was just trying to protect herself from this guy who she had deep feelings for but didn't completely trust. Six months later, my father asked her to marry him, but she said no. Six months after that, she turned him down again—even going so far as to start dating other guys—but he wouldn't go away. Finally, after two years and four proposals, my mother finally gave in and said yes, which makes me realize that this whole time, I've been focussing on what you've been saying to me rather than what you've actually been trying to communicate.

NILOUFAR: For you to save your life?

JOSH: No, not your actual words but the intentions behind your words. Don't you see? It was my name you let slip out to your boyfriend. Not Ben's. Not Drew's... Mine!

NILOUFAR: I told you, I was drunk.

JOSH: Which only confirms what I'm saying because it's when our guard is down that we reveal our true emotions.

NILOUFAR: But you're the one who's in danger, not them.

JOSH: I'm the one that has to change schools.

NILOUFAR: Exactly.

JOSH: You still don't get it?

NILOUFAR: Get what?

JOSH: You put me in danger because I'm the only one you really care about!

NILOUFAR: What?

JOSH: Unlike Ben, who's a door knob, or Drew, who's completely unavailable—in more ways than you think—I'm the only one who's treated you with any kind of respect and love. And unlike your fiancee, I'm probably not capable of putting two bullets through anyone's head, even if you cheat on me.

NILOUFAR: *(Taken aback; even surprisingly touched)* You... love me?

JOSH: You know that.

NILOUFAR: Oh.

JOSH: Does that scare you—to hear me say it—out loud?

NILOUFAR: No...I just don't feel the same way about you.

JOSH: Yes you do. You just don't know it yet.

NILOUFAR: No I don't.

JOSH: That's okay; I'd actually be worried at this point if you told me you did love me. What's important is what happened between us.

NILOUFAR: What happened?

JOSH: The moment our bodies came together—

NILOUFAR: It was just a fuck.

(JOSH is momentarily hurt by NILOUFAR's rejection, but overcomes the words by continuing to believe she really loves him.)

JOSH: *(Takes out a wad of money from his pocket)* So I've taken out my money for university—eleven thousand, eight hundred dollars. I also have a bunch of bonds and stocks that I haven't yet figured out how to cash-in without alerting my mother.

NILOUFAR: *(Disbelief)* You want to run away?

JOSH: It'll be enough to keep us going for a few months—help us get settled in another city. Or maybe we can even go to Mexico! It's so cheap to live down there and nobody ever finds you. The place is literally crawling with escaped convicts. I was down there last Christmas with my Dad—stayed in this small town right on the beach—a couple of dollars for a full meal with grilled fish, rice and beans—and you can sleep in hammocks looking up at the stars for almost nothing. You'll love it.

(NILOUFAR looks at JOSH a little differently.)

NILOUFAR: I like you, Josh, I think you're sweet… But you're a boy—

JOSH: I get my driver's license in eight months.

NILOUFAR: Will you listen to me? Watch my lips—

JOSH: It was my name you let slip out—

NILOUFAR: I'm not running away with you.

JOSH: I looked up your name; it means "water lily".

NILOUFAR: I don't love you.

JOSH: A guy who threatens to kill people? That's who you want to be with for the rest of your life?

NILOUFAR: I know it might sound weird to you, but he's just trying to protect me.

JOSH: And you show your appreciation for him by jerking off two guys in the boy's locker room.

NILOUFAR: Fine, so I'm a whore, is that what you want me to say?

JOSH: Falling for the dumbest guy in the class—

NILOUFAR: I'm allowed to make bad choices.

JOSH: No, Niloufar, you have no choices—that's the point! That's why you've been doing what you've been doing. When you graduate high school—

NILOUFAR: *(Blocking him out)* I can do whatever I want!

JOSH: You know very well that goon will be your husband whether you like it or not.

NILOUFAR: Nobody can force me to do anything!

JOSH: And if he's anything like he is now, you better believe he's going to beat you, cheat on you... Because behavior like that indicates to me that he might even try to—

NILOUFAR: I told you, I get to make the final decision!!!

*(*JOSH *looks at* NILOUFAR *with pity. She breaks down and starts sobbing. After a moment, he moves in to comfort her. Before he can take hold of her, she flings herself into his arms, and holds him tight, sobbing, like she'll never let go.)*

JOSH: It's okay...I'm here... They can't do this to you...I won't let it happen...

NILOUFAR: *(Slowly pulling herself together)* He'll kill you.

JOSH: Let him try...I mean, obviously I prefer to live, but if that's the cost of defending you, it's worth it. *(Trying to be humorous)*

I just don't want to be paralyzed.

NILOUFAR: *(Finding humor)* You're crazy.

JOSH: I fully admit it.

NILOUFAR: *(Releases herself from him)* So what are we supposed to do?

JOSH: Leave.

NILOUFAR: Just...?

JOSH: Go home after school, pack a small bag— ...What time do your parents go to sleep?

NILOUFAR: Ten.

JOSH: I'll come by at eleven tonight in a taxi to pick you up.

NILOUFAR: Tonight?! That's way too soon.

JOSH: We have no choice.

NILOUFAR: But where will we go?

JOSH: I have an uncle in Toronto; he always said if I ever got into any trouble, I could just show up at his door—no questions asked. We'll be safe there until we can figure out where to go from there.

NILOUFAR: I thought we were going to go to Mexico!

JOSH: We will. But Mexico's a big country. We got to plan it out right. Do you have a passport?

NILOUFAR: My parents keep it somewhere. Maybe we should wait?

JOSH: No. Find it. We have to go tonight. What street do you live on?

NILOUFAR: Rue Azilda.

JOSH: Where's that?

NILOUFAR: Ville D'Anjou?

JOSH: Where's that?

NILOUFAR: East.

JOSH: North East or South East?

NILOUFAR: Forget it—

JOSH: No, no, I'll find it. What's the cross street?

NILOUFAR: Chateauneuf…

JOSH: Write it on my hand. I might forget.

(NILOUFAR *writes it on* JOSH*'s palm.)*

JOSH: Perfect.

NILOUFAR: I can't believe we're thinking about doing this.

JOSH: We *are* doing this.

NILOUFAR: …Okay, we're doing this…I feel like I'm in a spy movie.

JOSH: Eleven o'clock. We'll catch the overnight bus to Toronto.

NILOUFAR: What about the train?

JOSH: We have to budget.

NILOUFAR: I'm shaking.

JOSH: Is that good?

NILOUFAR: I think so.

JOSH: Kiss me.

(NILOUFAR *kisses* JOSH.)

JOSH: I love you—and you don't have to say anything back.
(He starts to back out.)

NILOUFAR: Don't be late—I have nosy neighbors.

JOSH: *(Reading his palm; on Cloud 9)* Azilda and Chateauneuf.

*(*JOSH *runs off.* NILOUFAR *takes a big breath as if to tell herself that she can do this. After a few seconds, she starts to leave but* BEN *enters, preparing to have a smoke, surprised to find her there.)*

BEN: Nilou…

NILOUFAR: Oh, hi.

BEN: Was there another time we were supposed to…?

NILOUFAR: No.

BEN: Because I just saw Josh—

NILOUFAR: Yeah, I know.

BEN: You two weren't…

NILOUFAR: Definitely not.

BEN: Because nobody told me about another time.

NILOUFAR: There wasn't one.

BEN: Then what were you two doing here?

NILOUFAR: Talking.

BEN: Talking…

NILOUFAR: Yeah.

BEN: About what?

NILOUFAR: School stuff. Up-coming tests, position papers…I lost one of my text books and wanted to see if I could photocopy his so I wouldn't have to buy a new one.

BEN: Why'd you have to meet here?

NILOUFAR: Privacy; there's copyright issues.

BEN: Oh.

NILOUFAR: Yeah… So—

BEN: Is there something going on between you two?

NILOUFAR: No.

BEN: Because I just wanted to say, I'm sorry about what happened to your skirt.

NILOUFAR: It was nothing—like you said, came right out in the wash.

BEN: Yeah, I know, but I should've—

NILOUFAR: It's fine.

BEN: You just got me really excited—

NILOUFAR: Don't worry about it.

BEN: Hopefully you can see it as a compliment.

NILOUFAR: A compliment?

BEN: That I couldn't control myself with you.

NILOUFAR: Right…

BEN: And if you want, we can do more stuff together.

NILOUFAR: As I said—

BEN: Yeah, I know what you said, but why were you down here with Josh?

NILOUFAR: I already told you—

BEN: It's only fair that you treat us both equally…I can be romantic too.

NILOUFAR: Look, Ben, I got to go—

(More desperate; lightly grabbing NILOUFAR*'s arm as she tries to pass him:)*

BEN: Just give me another chance.

NILOUFAR: *(Staring at his hand on her arm; forcefully)* Take your hand off me.

*(Almost not understanding the severity of his action—but now aware of it—*BEN *takes his hand off* NILOUFAR *and steps aside.)*

NILOUFAR: Nobody touches my body unless I want them to. Is that clear?

*(*BEN *bows his head in shame;* NILOUFAR *exits with poise.)*

(Fade to black)

Scene 7

*(*BEN *and* DREW *are sitting on the floor of the shower room, smoking a cigarette.)*

BEN: Fucked up…

DREW: It's like— …I don't know.

BEN: I know.

DREW: *(Feeling guilty)* I mean, if it didn't happen now it probably would've happened later…

BEN: You think?

DREW: For sure. Something like that—it's almost destiny.

BEN: You mean it was meant to happen this way?

DREW: Did I say that?

BEN: No.

DREW: Then don't say that I said that.

*(*BEN *and* DREW *smoke.)*

BEN: Should we open a window?

DREW: Nobody's going to give a shit today. I heard they might even be sending everyone home after lunch.

BEN: I think I saw a T V reporter's truck parked outside.

DREW: That could also be for the break in.

BEN: When did that happen?

DREW: Also last night. They didn't take anything, but it clearly looked like someone broke the office window to get in.

BEN: Maybe someone was trying to steal a test.

DREW: Don't look at me.

BEN: Well, don't look at *me*.

*(*BEN *and* DREW *smoke.)*

DREW: Just better hope nobody said anything.

BEN: Who's going to say something?

DREW: I don't know, but they're definitely going to be doing some investigating.

BEN: Should that concern us?

DREW: What do you think?

BEN: But we didn't do anything.

DREW: Doesn't matter. Cops like to dig—that's what they do after something like this. Question everybody, follow every lead, piece things together… Make sure they don't miss anything.

BEN: *(With concern)* …Shit.

DREW: I sure the hell didn't say anything.

BEN: Me neither.

DREW: *(Suspicious of* BEN*)* You sure?

BEN: Yeah…I mean I might've mentioned something about the hand job to Jordan and Brant but—

DREW: What?!

BEN: They're not going to say anything.

DREW: How do you know?

BEN: They promised.

DREW: You're such an idiot.

BEN: I am not.

DREW: What else did you tell them?

BEN: Nothing about you, I swear.

DREW: Do you know what's going to happen when those dweebs get interrogated—a couple of cops with guns in their holsters breathing down their necks?

BEN: I still don't understand how we can get in trouble for this.

DREW: Maybe not jail trouble, but other trouble. People will blame us.

BEN: But all we did was have a little fun.

*(*JOSH *enters.)*

JOSH: Fun, right—passing her around like a piece of meat.

BEN: You weren't exactly sitting in the bleachers, if I remember.

JOSH: That's different; we had a connection.

BEN: Oh right, true love—between her hand and my dick.

JOSH: Which barely qualifies as anything, from what she told me.

BEN: That's such bull shit.

DREW: *(Steps in between them)* Would you two shut the fuck up! ...Regardless of how we treated her she had to be pretty messed up before anything happened with us. I mean anyone who pours gasoline all over their body and lights it on fire is NOT operating with a full deck.

JOSH: You actually believe she did that to herself?

DREW: Why shouldn't I?

BEN: It's what everyone's been saying.

JOSH: That's bull shit!

DREW: How do you know?

JOSH: I know.

BEN: Like you got some kind of special E S P connection to her spirit?

JOSH: No.

DREW: *(Sensing he knows more)* Then what?

JOSH: ...We were supposed to run away together.

DREW: When?

JOSH: Last night. It was all arranged. I was supposed to pick her up in a taxi and we were going to go stay with my uncle in Toronto.

DREW: Why would you do that?

JOSH: Her boyfriend threatened to kill me.

DREW: What boyfriend?

JOSH: She had a boyfriend. In university. They were supposed to get married after she graduated.

DREW: Where are you getting all this from?

JOSH: It was all arranged—she had no choice.

BEN: Nobody threatened to kill me.

JOSH: She only mentioned my name. Guy called my house and said he was going to put two bullets in my head if I showed up at school.

DREW: So, what, you're saying her boyfriend had something to do with this?

JOSH: Boyfriend. Parents. Who knows, maybe the whole fucking street! ...I know there is no way she would do this to herself.

BEN: So, now he thinks he's a private eye.

DREW: Does anyone else know about this?

JOSH: Of course not—she was scared shitless... We have to go to police and tell them everything.

DREW: Wow, wow, wow—

BEN: That ain't happening.

DREW: If you want to be some big hero, that's fine. Just don't involve us.

BEN: Yeah, we weren't the ones who were going to run away with her.

JOSH: If I don't tell them everything and then they find out, it's really going to look bad.

DREW: How's anyone going to find out? We haven't told anyone, did you?

JOSH: No.

DREW: So there's no problem.

(Beat)

JOSH: Jordan seemed to know something.

*(*DREW *looks at* BEN.*)*

BEN: *(To* DREW*)* I swear, I didn't mention your name.

DREW: Well, you mentioned his.

BEN: Yeah, of course, I mean he was in the room with me—that's half the story.

JOSH: *(Turning to* DREW*)* Come on, Drew... It's the right thing to do.

DREW: It's just I'm already on probation—any of this gets out and I'm definitely out of here.

BEN: That's nothing. Think of our pictures plastered all over the news. They'll make us out to be perverts or something.

DREW: I don't want to lose Jamie.

JOSH: Jamie? You're worried about losing Jamie?

BEN: I mean, come on Josh, she's toast anyway. It's not like anything we do is going to bring her back.

(JOSH swallows his rage at BEN.)

JOSH: Fine…I guess I'll just have to tell them everything myself.

DREW: Nobody's going to believe you.

BEN: We'll deny it.

(BEN gives JOSH a smug smile. The ball is back in JOSH's court. He ponders…)

JOSH: I'll just have to take my chances.

DREW: *(Posturing)* I wouldn't advise it if I were you.

BEN: *(Joining him)* I agree.

(BEN and DREW block off JOSH's exit. He counters…)

JOSH: I saw you.

DREW: You saw what?

JOSH: You know exactly.

BEN: Can you believe the nerve of this guy—

JOSH: *(With force)* I saw you two getting it on!

(Beat)

DREW: What are you talking about?

JOSH: I fucking know, all right? You, down on your knees, Ben's dick in your mouth.

BEN: *(Nervous)* That's a really sick imagination you got there.

JOSH: I got a picture.

BEN: That's bull shit.

JOSH: We all go to the cops and tell them exactly what happened, or I swear to God, that picture is going to go viral.

(Suddenly, BEN *lunges at* JOSH *and starts beating him up.* DREW *just hangs back but sees that it is starting to get dangerous.)*

DREW: All right, that's enough… Let him go… Let go …Ben!

*(*BEN *backs off and defiantly* JOSH *stands up and faces him, with a bloodied lip.)*

JOSH: Don't you understand? I loved her! What's so wrong with that—

*(*BEN *charges* JOSH *and smashes him hard into the shower wall.* JOSH *hits his head on the faucet and slides down the wall into a sitting position, looking like something terrible has happened to his spine.)*

DREW: What the fuck did you do that for?!

BEN: *(To* JOSH*)* I am NOT fucking gay!!!

JOSH: *(Struggling to speak)* I can't… Help, I can't move my…

DREW: Shit!

BEN: He shouldn't have said that.

JOSH: Please…

DREW: *(Panicked)* Oh my God… What do we do?

BEN: *(Almost appearing to be the leader now)* Let's get the fuck out of here.
(He runs out.)

JOSH: I won't tell… Just, please…

*(*DREW *thinks about helping him, but panics and leaves too.* JOSH *struggles to breath, and is unable to move his limbs.)*

JOSH: *(Trying to yell)* Help… Somebody… Help…

(Suddenly, NILOUFAR *enters from the right side of the stage— [not the real entrance] —and is dressed in a light jacket, rolling a small suitcase as in the Prologue.)*

(In this world, it is the evening before, and she has just arrived on a street corner, looking out for a taxi, but also checking to make sure none of the neighbors are watching her.)

JOSH: Nilou...

*(*NILOUFAR *is oblivious to* JOSH *as she looks out for the taxi. A car approaches, but then passes by.)*

NILOUFAR: *(To herself)* Come on... Where are you?

JOSH: My hands started to sweat... The ink got all smudged...

*(*NILOUFAR *looks at her watch and notes the time, becoming increasingly nervous.)*

JOSH: I even went back to the school... Broke into the office for your address...

(Another car approaches and comes to a stop in front of her: NILOUFAR *smiles in anticipation, going toward the car with her suitcase.)*

JOSH: By the time I got to you...

(When the door to the car opens, NILOUFAR *is horrified and immediately changes direction, trying to run away.)*

(Quick black out)

NILOUFAR: Hel(p)—

(Something like Not Ready To Love *by Rufus Wainwright plays.)*

END OF PLAY

www.ingramcontent.com/pod-product-compliance
Lightning Source LLC
Chambersburg PA
CBHW052220090426
42741CB00010B/2622

9780881458824